Chutneys for All

Easy Canning and Preserving Recipes

Contents

Introduction 4

Recipe 1. Spicy peach chutney 7

Recipe 2. Cranberry chutney I 10

Recipe 3. Spiced cranberry chutney......................12

Recipe 4. Cranberry, apple, and fresh ginger chutney
....15

Recipe 5. Apple thyme chutney 18

Recipe 6. Tomato chutney 20

Recipe 7. Tomato and peach chutney 23

Recipe 8. Mint Chutney II.....................................25

Recipe 9. Tomato chutney 27

Recipe 10. Green mango chutney 29

Recipe 11. Mango chutney II 32

Recipe 12. Cherry Chutney 35

Recipe 13. Apricot cranberry chutney 38

Recipe 14. Roasted pear and mango chutney 41

Recipe 15. Mango chutney III...............................44

Recipe 16. Mint chutney 46

Recipe 17. Easy cranberry sauce...........................48

Recipe 18. Apple chutney 50

Recipe 19. Sweet tamarind chutney......................52

Recipe 20. Green chutney 55

Recipe 21. Onion chutney 57

Recipe 22. Spiced apple chutney 59

Recipe 23. Cilantro chutney 62
Recipe 24. Coconut chutney 64
Recipe 25. Sweet tomato chutney 66
Recipe 26. Mango chutney 68
Recipe 27. Peanut cilantro chutney 71
Recipe 28. Mango-Pineapple chutney 73
Recipe 29. Killer cranberry chutney 76
Recipe 30. Spiced cranberry and apple chutney 78

Introduction

Delight Your Family and Friends with Delicious Chutneys for All Occasions!

Are you looking to create mouthwatering chutney that your family and friends will relish?

Do you want easy, delicious recipes that take minimal preparation, with long-term storage options?

Are you ready to experience a world of flavor with the help of amazing canning and preserving recipes?

Then this is the perfect cookbook for you.

This delightful cookbook of chutney recipes is an excellent guide to the unique and diverse flavors that can be created in the home kitchen. Filled with simple, easy to follow recipes, this book is sure to please and inspire. Covering a wide variety of styles, such as sweet and spicy chutneys, this cookbook is a great resource for anyone interested in the exciting flavors and culinary techniques involved in creating chutney.

This cookbook contains:

- Delicious collection of easy-to-prepare chutney recipes, perfect for every season
- Explore recipes for small batches of preserves-no need for a large space-taking canner
- Ingredients used are easy to find and perfect for anyone looking for unique flavors
- Step-by-step instructions from making the preserve to storing it
- Includes photos to accompany each recipe

So, start discovering the amazing world of chutney with this handy cookbook and let your imagination run wild with the endless possibilities that canning and preserving offer.

Get Your copy Today!

Recipe 1. Spicy peach chutney

Preparation Time-20 minutes

Servings –96

Ingredients:

1. 2 minced cloves garlic
2. 1 teaspoon curry powder
3. 2 ounces pickling spice
4. 32 ounces packed brown sugar
5. 4 ounces chopped onion

6. 1/2 ounce mustard seed
7. 8 ounces raisins
8. 32 ounces apple cider vinegar
9. 5 ounces chopped preserved ginger
10. 64 ounces peeled and sliced peaches
11. 3/4 ounce chili powder

Instructions:

Step 1   Stir all ingredients except for pickling spice in a large heavy stockpot. Wrap pickling spice in a cheesecloth bag and place in the mixture in the pot.

Step 2   Bring the mixture to a boil, reduce heat to medium and cook for 90 minutes until chutney reaches a desired consistency. Often stir to prevent scorching.

Step 3   Remove a cheesecloth bag from the mixture and transfer to hot jars that have been sterilized. Seal jars and process according to canners' manufacturer instructions.

Recipe 2. Cranberry chutney I

Preparation Time-20 minutes

Servings –20

Ingredients:

1. 12 ounces fresh cranberries
2. 1/2 teaspoon ground cinnamon
3. 8 ounces peeled, diced, and cored apples
4. 1/4 teaspoon ground ginger
5. 4 ounces raisins

6. 4 ounces cider vinegar
7. 6 ounces white sugar
8. 1/8 teaspoon ground cloves
9. 1/4 teaspoon ground allspice
10. 8 ounces water

Instructions:

Step 1　Bring water and white sugar to a boil in a medium saucepan on medium heat.

Step 2　Stir in the rest of the ingredients, bring to a boil again, and simmer for 10 minutes. Stir frequently.

Step 3　Remove the pan from heat and transfer mixture to a bowl. Wrap with plastic while leaving enough slack to let wrap touch the surface of the liquid. Let stand until cooled completely and serve.

Recipe 3. Spiced cranberry chutney

Preparation Time-30 minutes

Servings –10

Ingredients:

1. 2 ounces finely chopped dried apricots
2. 1 peeled, cored, and chopped Granny Smith apple
3. 2 ounces fresh lemon juice
4. 1/2 teaspoon red pepper flakes

5. 8 ounces water
6. 4 ounces raisins
7. 24 ounces fresh cranberries
8. 1 teaspoon grated lemon zest
9. 2 ounces chopped crystallized ginger
10. 4 ounces brown sugar

Instructions:

Step 1 Mix apricots, sugar, water, and raisins in a large saucepan. Bring to a boil on the medium high heat.

Step 2 Reduce the heat to medium-to-low and then simmer for 5 minutes.

Step 3 Stir in berries, apple, and zest and simmer for 10 more minutes.

Step 4 Add the rest of the ingredients, stir, and remove the pan from heat. Chill overnight and pour into jars to store or serve.

Recipe 4. Cranberry, apple, and fresh ginger chutney

Preparation Time -15minutes

Servings –8

Ingredients:

1. 32 ounces fresh cranberries
2. 4 ounces white sugar
3. 1 teaspoon fresh minced ginger root
4. 4 ounces finely chopped celery

5. 6 ounces packed brown sugar
6. 8 ounces water
7. 8 ounces raisins
8. 4 ounces chopped Granny Smith apple
9. 1/4 teaspoon ground cloves
10. 1/3 ounce ground cinnamon
11. 4 ounces minced onion

Instructions:

Step 1 Mix cranberries, raisins, sugar, ginger, cinnamon, ginger root, cloves, and water in a large pan and bring to a boil on medium high.

Step 2 Reduce heat to low and simmer for 5 minutes until berries burst.

Step 3 Stir in onion, apple, and celery and cook for 5-10 minutes until mixture thickens.

Step 4 Pour into a sealable container and chill overnight. Store in jars or serve.

Recipe 5. Apple thyme chutney

Preparation Time-20 minutes

Servings –6

Ingredients:

1. 1 ounce apple cider vinegar
2. 3 peeled, cored, and chopped large apples
3. 1 ounce apple brandy
4. 2 ounces white sugar
5. ½ ounce ground thyme

6.   1 bay leaf

7.   a pinch salt

Instructions:

Step 1   Mix all ingredients except for brandy and salt in a medium saucepan on medium low heat. Partially cover the pan and simmer the mixture for 1 hour until thick and sticky. Add the brandy 5-10 minutes before the end of the cooking time and stir well. Season with salt.

Step 2   Spoon chutney into hot sterilized jars and seal according to canners' instructions. Cool and place in a refrigerator before using. Remove bay leaf before using.

Recipe 6. Tomato chutney

Preparation Time-20 minutes

Servings –12

Ingredients:

1. 2 chopped tomatoes
2. a pinch of asafetida powder
3. 2 chopped green chili peppers
4. salt
5. 1/2 ounce cooking oil

6. 1/2 chopped onion
7. 2 ounces chopped cilantro leaves
8. 1 teaspoon mustard seed
9. 4 dried red chili peppers
10. 1 teaspoon skinned and split black lentils
11. 1/2 ounce cooking oil

Instructions:

Step 1   Heat oil in a small frying pan on medium heat and sauté lentils, mustard, and red chili peppers in the oil until mustard seeds popped.

Step 2   Remove the pan from heat and stir in green peppers and asafetida powder. Remove the pan from heat and cool slightly.

Step 3   Transfer mixture in the pan to a mortar and pestle, then grind into a fine powder.

Step 4   Return the frying pan to heat with 1/2 ounce of oil and sauté onion in the oil for 5 minutes until tender.

Step 5   Add tomatoes and stir well, cook for 3 minutes until the liquid has evaporated.

Step 6   Add tomato mixture to the lentils and grind again until onions are completely smashed. Season with salt.

Step 7   Fold cilantro into the chutney and serve.

Recipe 7. Tomato and peach chutney

Preparation Time-35 minutes

Servings –64

Ingredients:

1. 1/2 ounce salt
2. 4 diced medium onions
3. 5 peeled, chopped, and pitted fresh peaches

4. 8 ounces pickling spice, wrapped in cheesecloth
5. 15 peeled and chopped tomatoes
6. 12 ounces distilled white vinegar
7. 5 peeled, diced, and cored red apples
8. 4 diced stalks celery

Instructions:

Step 1   Mix all ingredients in a huge pot and boil on medium heat.

Step 2   Lower the heat and cook for a further 2 hours, just until the desired thickness is reached. Remove the pan from the heat and allow it to cool. Fill jars halfway with the mixture and store in plastic containers in the refrigerator or freezer.

Recipe 8. Mint Chutney II

Preparation Time-10 minutes

Servings –6

Ingredients:

1. 4 ounces fresh mint leaves
2. 1/2 ounce fresh lemon juice
3. 2 fresh green chili peppers
4. 1 teaspoon salt
5. 1 onion, cut in quarters

Instructions:

Step 1   Place all ingredients in a blender and process until smooth. Remove and serve or store in jars.

Recipe 9. Tomato chutney

Preparation Time-15 minutes

Servings –8

Ingredients:

1. 1 teaspoon minced garlic
2. 16 ounces chopped tomatoes
3. 1/3 ounce grated ginger
4. 1 ounce chopped cilantro
5. 1/3 ounce chili powder

6. A pinch of salt
7. 1/2 ounce white sugar

Instructions:

Step 1   Combine all ingredients in a saucepan on medium heat and cook for 10 minutes until thick and saucy. Remove from heat and let it cool before storing or serving.

Recipe 10. Green mango chutney

Preparation Time-40minutes

Servings –32

Ingredients:

1. 8 ounces cider vinegar
2. 1/2 ounce black pepper
3. 6 minced cloves garlic
4. 2 ounces finely chopped serrano peppers
5. 3/4 ounce fresh minced ginger root

6. 4 ounces raisins
7. 1/4 ounce lemon zest
8. 8 ounces water
9. 1 ounce molasses
10. 4 whole cloves
11. 1 small cinnamon stick
12. 32 ounces unripened green mango, peeled, seeded, and diced

Instructions:

Step 1   Place all ingredients in a large saucepan and bring to a boil on medium high. Reduce heat to medium low and simmer for 30 minutes until the mixture reaches a jam-like consistency.

Step 2   Stir often. Remove from heat once desired consistency is reached and cool.

Step 3   Store chutney in the refrigerator in glass jars or the freezer in plastic containers.

Recipe 11. Mango chutney II

Preparation Time-25 minutes

Servings –24

Ingredients:

1. 4 peeled and seeded green unripened mangoes, sliced into strips
2. 5 crushed black peppercorns
3. 1/2 teaspoon red pepper flakes
4. 20 ounces white sugar

5. 1 teaspoon salt
6. 1 chopped piece fresh ginger root
7. 1 teaspoon cumin seed
8. 2 cardamom pods
9. 8 ounces distilled white vinegar
10. 1 cinnamon stick
11. 5 whole cloves
12. 3 peeled cloves garlic
13. 4 cardamom seeds

Instructions:

Step 1   Place ginger and garlic in a mortar and pestle, then crush until a paste forms. Place mangoes in a large stockpot and stir ginger paste into the mangoes.

Step 2   Add the rest of the ingredients to the mango mixture except for vinegar and peppercorns. Stir and cover the pot. Let the pot stand at room temperature overnight.

Step 3   Bring pot to a simmer on medium heat and cook the mixture for 30 minutes until it starts to thicken. Add vinegar and peppercorns and cook for 1 minute. Remove from heat and cool before serving.

Recipe 12. Cherry Chutney

Preparation Time-30 minutes

Servings –12

Ingredients:

1. 2 ounces brown sugar
2. 1 large, chopped onion
3. 1/4 teaspoon ground nutmeg
4. 1 teaspoon salt
5. 8 ounces cider vinegar

6. 1 ounce minced fresh ginger
7. 1 peeled, chopped, and cored Granny Smith apple
8. 16 ounces pitted cherries
9. 4 ounces rice vinegar
10. 2 ounces white sugar
11. 1 ounce Chinese five-spice powder

Instructions:

Step 1   Put all the ingredients in a big saucepan and then bring to a simmer on the medium high heat. Reduce the heat to the medium low then simmer, then cover the pan and simmer for 60 minutes. Stir often.

Step 2   Remove lid and keep simmering until you have a desired consistency. Remove from heat and let it cool to a room temperature before storing in jars. Place in a refrigerator and chill before serving.

Recipe 13. Apricot cranberry chutney

Preparation Time-10 minutes

Servings –12

Ingredients:

1. 4 ounces raisins
2. 8 ounces water
3. 1/4 teaspoon ground allspice
4. 2 ounces diced and dried apricots

5. 3/4 teaspoon ground cinnamon
6. 6 ounces white sugar
7. 12 ounces fresh cranberries
8. 4 ounces cider vinegar
9. a pinch of ground cloves
10. 1/4 teaspoon ground ginger

Instructions:

Step 1 Combine apricots, raisins, cranberries, cinnamon, ginger, cloves, and allspice in a large bowl.

Step 2 Bring water and sugar to a boil in a medium pan on medium heat. Stir in the fruit and cider vinegar, then bring to a boil.

Step 3 Reduce heat and simmer for 10 minutes. Remove pan from heat and let stand for 5 minutes.

Step 4 Serve chutney right away or transfer to a sealable container and place in the refrigerator.

Recipe 14. Roasted pear and mango chutney

Preparation Time-30 minutes

Servings –122

Ingredients:

1. 6 ounces cider vinegar
2. 1 teaspoon ground cinnamon
3. 1 ounce vegetable oil
4. 4 ounces dried sour cherries

5. 1 small chopped red onion
6. 1/2 ounce cayenne pepper
7. 2 chopped clove garlic
8. 1/2 ounce brown sugar
9. 2 ounces maple syrup
10. 1 ounce lemon juice
11. 16 ounces diced unripened green mango
12. 1 teaspoon fresh grated ginger
13. 1 chopped green chili pepper
14. 2 ounces brown sugar
15. 2 firm peeled and cored green pears, cut in half

Instructions:

Step 1 Preheat an oven to 350 degrees Fahrenheit. Coat a baking sheet with cooking oil.

Step 2 Mix lemon juice, cinnamon, and 1/2 ounce of brown sugar. Toss pears in the mixture until coated and place on the baking sheet with the cut side down. Brush pears with oil and place in the oven for 40-50 minutes until tender and caramelized.

Step 3 Remove pears from the oven and cool on a wire rack.

Step 4   In the meantime, combine the rest of the ingredients in a medium saucepan and bring to a boil. Reduce heat and simmer for 35-40 minutes until mangoes are translucent and liquid reaches the consistency of a syrup.

Step 5   Remove pan from heat and cool.

Step 6   Chop pears and mix in with mango in a large bowl. Cover the bowl and chill for 24 hours.

Recipe 15. Mango chutney III

Preparation Time-20 minutes

Servings –10

Ingredients:

1. 1/2 seeded and chopped habanero pepper
2. 1/2 teaspoon salt
3. 3 chopped sprigs fresh cilantro
4. 1/2 ounce lime juice
5. 1 peeled, chopped, and seeded mango

6. 3 chopped cloves garlic

Instructions:

Step 1   Combine all ingredients in a blender and process until smooth and desired thickness. Serve or store in a refrigerator.

Recipe 16. Mint chutney

Preparation Time-10 minutes

Servings –8

Ingredients:

1. 1/2 ounce lemon juice
2. 1/2 teaspoon salt
3. 2 ounces water
4. 1 bunch fresh cilantro
5. 1 green chili pepper

6. 12 ounces fresh mint leaves

7. 1 medium onion, cut into chunks

Instructions:

Step 1   Combine all ingredients except for water in a food processor and purée until a fine paste forms. Add enough water to reach a desired thickness.

Recipe 17. Easy cranberry sauce

Preparation Time-15 minutes

Servings –8

Ingredients:

1. 16 ounces white sugar
2. 1 ounce ground cinnamon
3. 4 ounces pitted fresh cherries, cut in half
4. 12 ounces fresh cranberries
5. 20 ounces white wine

6. a pinch ground ginger

Instructions:

Step 1 Mix all ingredients except for cranberries and cherries in a medium saucepan and bring to simmer on medium-high heat. Stir until sugar is dissolved.

Step 2 Add cranberries and cherries and return the mixture to simmer. Reduce heat to medium low, cover the pan and cook for 45 minutes. Stir often.

Step 3 Remove pan from heat and place into a refrigerator until fully chilled.

Recipe 18. Apple chutney

Preparation Time-20 minutes

Servings –40

Ingredients:

1. 1/2 tsp ground cardamom
2. 1 yellow onion, cut in quarters
3. 3 peeled pieces fresh ginger root, 1 each
4. 1/2 tsp white pepper
5. 8 ounces white wine vinegar

6. 1/4 tsp ground nutmeg
7. 1/2 tsp ground cinnamon
8. 4 ounces brown sugar
9. 15 cored, peeled, and finely chopped Granny Smith apples
10. 4 ounces white sugar

Instructions:

Step 1   Combine all ingredients in a saucepan and bring to boil on the med-high heat. And reduce to the medium heat then simmer for 30 minutes. Stir often and simmer until apples are tender. Add water to keep the mixture moist.

Step 2   Remove onion and ginger, then let mixture stand until slightly cooled. Store in the refrigerator until ready to serve.

Recipe 19. Sweet tamarind chutney

Preparation Time-15 minutes

Servings –10

Ingredients:

1. 16 ounces water
2. 1/2 tsp garam masala
3. 1 ½ ounces tamarind paste
4. 1/2 tsp asafetida powder
5. 1 tsp ground ginger

6. 10 ounces white sugar
7. 1/2 ounce canola oil
8. 1 teaspoon cumin seeds
9. 1/2 tsp cayenne pepper
10. 1/2 tsp fennel seeds

Instructions:

Step 1 Heat canola oil in a pan on medium heat and sauté cumin, ginger, pepper, garam masala, asafetida powder, and fennel in the oil for 2 minutes.

Step 2 Add water, sugar, and tamarind paste into the mixture and stir. Bring to a boil on medium high heat.

Step 3 Reduce heat to low and simmer for 20-30 minutes until mixture turns deep brown and thick enough to coat spoon's back. Remove pan from heat and cool the mixture until it reaches a desired thickness.

Recipe 20. Green chutney

Preparation Time-20 minutes

Servings –4

Ingredients:

1. 1 hot green minced chili pepper
2. 1/2 ounce fresh minced ginger root
3. 1 clove garlic
4. 1 bunch fresh cilantro
5. salt

6. 1/2 ounce peanuts

7. 1 ounce lemon juice

Instructions:

Step 1   Place all ingredients in a blender and process until smooth. Add water if the mixture is too dry. Store in a refrigerator until ready to serve.

Recipe 21. Onion chutney

Preparation Time-20 minutes

Servings –4

Ingredients:

1. 1/2 teaspoon salt
2. 1 teaspoon white sugar
3. 1 teaspoon paprika
4. 1 minced sweet onion
5. 1 ½ ounces white vinegar

6. 1/2 teaspoon cayenne pepper

7. 1/2 ounce ketchup

Instructions:

Step 1   Combine all ingredients in a medium bowl until smooth.

Recipe 22. Spiced apple chutney

Preparation Time-15 minutes

Servings –10

Ingredients:

1. 1/4 teaspoon Aleppo pepper flakes
2. 1/2 teaspoon yellow mustard seed
3. 4 peeled and cored tart apples, cubed (1/2)
4. 12 ounces white sugar
5. 5 thick slices fresh ginger

6. 2 minced garlic cloves
7. 1 whole star anise
8. 12 ounces white vinegar
9. 2 ounces diced shallots
10. 2 ounces diced and dried apricots
11. 1 teaspoon kosher salt
12. 2 ounces golden raisins

Instructions:

Step 1   Place vinegar and sugar in large saucepan and whisk until well combined. Stir in apples, apricots, star anise, raisins, shallots, pepper flakes, and ginger. Bring mixture to simmer on med-high heat. Reduce the heat to the medium low and stir in the rest of the ingredients.

Step 2   Simmer for 45 minutes until liquid has reduced and fruit is tender. Remove pan from heat, then take out ginger and star anise. Pour the mixture into a bowl and chill for 60 minutes. Season with salt and pepper and serve or transfer into jars.

Recipe 23. Cilantro chutney

Preparation Time-20 minutes

Servings –14

Ingredients:

1. 1 teaspoon cumin seeds
2. 2 bunches fresh cilantro, leaves picked from stems
3. 1 ounce tomato sauce
4. 1 ounce lemon juice

5. 1 ounce minced fresh ginger root
6. 2 green chili peppers
7. 1/2 ounce water

Instructions:

Step 1 Place all ingredients in a blender and process until finely ground. Stir water into the mixture until the sauce of the desired consistency is made.

Recipe 24. Coconut chutney

Preparation Time-20 minutes

Servings –8

Ingredients:

1. 1/4 teaspoon cumin seeds
2. 1/2 teaspoon of mustard seed
3. 1/2 ounce vegetable oil
4. 3 fresh chopped red chili peppers
5. 1/2 drained and grated fresh whole coconut

6. 4 ounces plain yogurt

Instructions:

Step 1   Combine coconut and yogurt in a blender and process until a paste forms. Transfer the mixture to a bowl.

Step 2   Heat vegetable oil in a medium pan on medium heat and sauté chili peppers, mustard, and cumin seeds in the oil until mustard seeds start to burst and pop. Spoon mixture from the saucepan over the coconut mixture. Cover the bowl and chill until ready to serve or store in a sealable container.

Recipe 25. Sweet tomato chutney

Preparation Time-15 minutes

Servings –8

Ingredients:

1. 1/2 teaspoon Indian black salt
2. 4 ounces grated palm sugar
3. 1 peeled piece fresh ginger root
4. 2 bay leaves
5. 1/2 teaspoon cumin seeds

6. 1 dried red chili, cut in half
7. 4 chopped pitted dates
8. 4 cubed tomatoes
9. 1 ounce vegetable oil

Instructions:

Step 1   Heat oil in a frying pan on medium heat and sauté seeds, bay leaves, and chili pepper in the oil for 1-2 minutes until seeds begin to pop.

Step 2   Add tomatoes and ginger to the cumin mixture and cook and stir for 5 minutes until all the liquid in the tomatoes evaporates.

Step 3   Stir in palm sugar and cook for 5 minutes until dissolved. Season with black salt.

Step 4   Remove ginger and bay leaves before serving chutney or storing.

Recipe 26. Mango chutney

Preparation Time-15 minutes

Servings-240

Ingredients:

1. 1/3 ounce ground ginger
2. 4 ounces chopped ginger root
3. 8 ounces golden raisins
4. 24 ounces distilled white vinegar
5. 48 ounces brown sugars

6. 2 large, chopped onions
7. 1 teaspoon ground cloves
8. 2/3 ounce ground allspice
9. 8 ounces raisins
10. 5 small seeded and chopped red hot chili peppers
11. 1 teaspoon ground cinnamon
12. 48 ounces white sugar
13. 1 teaspoon kosher salt
14. 3 chopped cloves garlic
15. 1/3 ounce ground nutmeg
16. 4 ounces sliced almonds
17. 128 ounces sliced semi-ripened mangos

Instructions:

Step 1 Combine white vinegar, both sugars, cinnamon, ginger, cloves, allspice, nutmeg, chili peppers, and salt in a large saucepan on medium high heat and bring to a boil. Boil for 30 minutes.

Step 2 Add all raisins, onions, garlic, and ginger, then stir and continue to boil for another 30 minutes.

Step 3   Stir in the last two ingredients, reduce heat to low and simmer for 30 minutes. Remove from heat and let the mixture cool before storing in jars and sealing.

Recipe 27. Peanut cilantro chutney

Preparation Time-20 minutes

Servings –28

Ingredients:

1. 1/2 ounce lemon juice
2. 2 seeded and chopped green chili peppers
3. 1/2 ounce cumin seeds
4. 16 ounces cilantro leaves
5. 12 ounces plain yogurt

6. 2 peeled garlic cloves
7. 8 ounces coarsely chopped roasted unsalted peanuts
8. salt

Instructions:

Step 1 Combine chili peppers, cumin, garlic, and cilantro in a food processor and purée into a fine paste. Add lemon juice and yogurt to the mixture and blend for 1-2 minutes until smooth.

Step 2 Stir in nuts and salt and serve or store.

Recipe 28. Mango-Pineapple chutney

Preparation Time-35 minutes

Servings –24

Ingredients:

1. 1 small peeled and diced pineapple
2. 3 large peeled, diced, and pitted ripened mangoes
3. 1 teaspoon crushed red pepper flakes

4. 4 ounces apple cider vinegar
5. 4 ounces brown sugar
6. 1 large minced sweet onion
7. 1 large diced yellow bell pepper
8. 4 peeled and minced piece ginger root
9. 3/4 ounce curry powder
10. 1 ounce vegetable oil

Instructions:

Step 1   Heat oil in a large pan on medium heat and sauté the pepper flakes in the oil until they sizzled. Add onion to the pepper flakes and stir.

Step 2   Reduce heat to low and cover the pan. Cook for 20 minutes until onions have softened. Stir frequently.

Step 3   Uncover the pan and turn heat up to medium. Add ginger and bell pepper and stir well. Cook for 2-3 minutes until fragrant.

Step 4   Stir in the rest of the ingredients and increase heat to simmer. Cook for 30 minutes while stirring frequently.

Step 5   Remove the pan from heat and cool before storing in a sealable container and placing in the refrigerator.

Recipe 29. Killer cranberry chutney

Preparation Time-25 minutes

Servings –12

Ingredients:

1. 2 peeled, chopped, and cored apples
2. 2 ounces apple cider vinegar
3. 1/2 teaspoon cinnamon, ground
4. 12 ounces cranberries
5. 1/2 minced red onions

6. 6 ounces white sugar
7. 1/2 ounce cooking oil
8. 2 ounces freshly squeezed orange juice
9. 2 peeled, chopped, and cored pears

Instructions:

Step 1   Heat cooking oil in a saucepan on medium heat and sauté onion for 2 -3 minutes in the oil until translucent. Stir in the rest of the ingredients except for apple and pear for 3-5 minutes.

Step 2   Add apple and pears, then cook for 10-15 minutes until cranberries are softened.

Recipe 30. Spiced cranberry and apple chutney

Preparation Time-15 minutes

Servings –48

Ingredients:

1. 1 large peeled, chopped, and cored Granny Smith apple
2. 1/4 teaspoon ground cloves
3. 16 ounces fresh cranberries

4. 1/2 teaspoon ground ginger
5. 2 finely chopped stalks celery
6. a pinch salt
7. 1 ½ ounces water
8. 16 ounces white sugar
9. ½ ounce grated orange zest
10. 8 ounces fresh orange juice
11. 8 ounces golden raisins
12. 2 ounces pecans

Instructions:

Step 1   Bring cranberries, white sugar, and water to a boil in a large pan on medium high heat. Reduce heat to medium and cook for 8-10 minutes until berries have burst.

Step 2   Stir in the rest of the ingredients and cook for 35 minutes until liquid is reduced and celery is softened.

Step 3   Remove pan from heat and let mixture stand for 15-20 minutes until thickened.

Printed in Great Britain
by Amazon